For Dom
—Jonah

To J.W.
—J.W.

Printed in Hong Kong
First Edition
1 3 5 7 9 10 8 6 4 2
This book is set in 16-pt. Cochin.

LIBRARY OF CONGRESS CATALOGING-IN-PUBLICATION DATA
Winter, Jonah.
Once upon a time in Chicago : the story of Benny Goodman
/ by Jonah Winter ; illustrated by Jeanette Winter
p. cm.
Summary: A simple biography of the great jazz musician, Benny Goodman,
and how his extraordinary musical ability was originally encouraged by
his immigrant father.
ISBN 0-7868-0462-9 (trade) — ISBN 0-7868-2404-2 (lib. bdg.)
1. Goodman, Benny, 1909—Juvenile literature.
2. Clarinetists—United States—Biography—Juvenile literature.
3. Jazz musicians—United States—Biography—Juvenile literature.
[1. Goodman, Benny, 1909– 2. Clarinetists.
3. Musicians. 4. Jazz.] I. Winter, Jeanette, ill

ML3930.G66 W56 2000   781.65'092-dc21   [B]
99-59954

Visit www.hyperionchildrensbooks.com

Benjamin David "Benny" Goodman was born in Chicago, Illinois, on May 30, 1909. In the 1930s, he assembled a band that featured the best black and white musicians of the era. Goodman was the first major bandleader to integrate his band. His bandstand sported an all-star lineup: the amazing Teddy Wilson at piano; the Original Master of the Vibes, Lionel Hampton; Gene Krupa on drums; and Ziggy Elman with his Jewish klezmer music trumpet playing.

His band combined dance-band orchestration with a "hot jazz" sound. It was groundbreaking music that swept through America over the radio airwaves—especially on Goodman's weekly radio show, *Let's Dance*. When audience members started dancing in the aisles of Goodman's New York Paramount Theater show in 1937, it was official—the Swing Era had begun! And Benny Goodman was dubbed The King of Swing.

Through his swing band, Goodman brought jazz to the masses as never before. And his historic Carnegie Hall performance on January 16, 1938, lifted jazz to unimaginable heights.

Goodman recorded dozens and dozens of albums—literally hundreds of hours of music. On June 13, 1986, Benny Goodman had a heart attack. Just before he died, he was playing his clarinet.

—Jonah Winter

Once there was a neighborhood in Chicago where immigrants from Russia lived. It was poor, but lively.

The streets were crowded with people buying and selling all sorts of things—pots and pans, fruits and vegetables, clothes.

There were horses, policemen, and
barrels and barrels of pickles.

Many signs were in Hebrew or
Russian. Up and down the streets, those
were the languages people spoke. It was
like a foreign country.

In the evenings people sat on their stoops. They talked and they talked. Their new lives were not easy.

But they always had one thing. They had music. Fiddlers and accordionists played songs from the old country.

They played on street corners, fire escapes, and rooftops.

In this neighborhood, there lived a good, hardworking Jewish man named David Goodman. He did his best to support his wife and family.

And what a huge family it was. He and
his wife, Dora, had twelve children! They
lived in a tiny, dark apartment. It was all
they could afford.

David Goodman worked long days and made little money. Sometimes he worked as a tailor in large factory shops.

As hard as he worked, he never made enough money to properly clothe his children.

David's wife, Dora, was always
mending her children's worn-out clothing.

David Goodman wanted his family to
have a better life. So, he took three of his
sons—Harry, Freddy, and Benny—to the
local synagogue. There was a boys' band
that played there. Maybe his sons could
learn to play.

The three boys were assigned
instruments according to their size.
Harry got a tuba. Freddy got a trumpet.
    And little Benny got the fanciest
instrument, a clarinet.

Benny was a quiet boy. Benny never had too much to say. He smiled politely a lot. He was the shyest kid in his fourth-grade class. But when Benny got home and opened up his clarinet case,

his eyes sparkled. The clarinet case was
lined with purple velvet. The clarinet itself
was black and shiny with silver keys.
What an instrument!

Benny liked playing the clarinet more than he liked talking. For a while, Benny's family couldn't keep him away from his instrument. His brothers and sisters made him practice on the fire escape.

His practice paid off. Before long, he was in a marching band. Benny's father was thrilled. He hoped Benny could grow up to make more money and have a better life.

Though he could scarcely afford it, David Goodman signed Benny up for some lessons with the great Franz Schoepp.

Benny practiced and practiced and practiced—scales, whole tones, and exercises from books. Franz Schoepp was training Benny to become a classical clarinetist, like himself.

But Benny loved a new kind of music
called jazz. Jazz was fun and hot, and it
made people want to get up and dance.
Benny listened to his brothers' jazz
records on a phonograph. He memorized
the clarinet solos note for note.

Benny heard about an "Amateur Night" at the Central Park Theater in downtown Chicago. People performed different acts. Benny brought his clarinet.

When he got up on stage, in front of a huge audience, Benny wasn't even nervous. He played his solos he had memorized. His tunes were a big hit!

A week later the phone rang. It was the theater owner. He asked Benny if he could fill in for someone that night.

Benny was there in a flash. In one hour, he made five dollars. It was more than his father made in a whole day.

Word got out about Benny. He got a call from a nightclub where a jazz band played. When he arrived, the bandleader asked if Benny could play a difficult song.

Not only could Benny play it—he played it sixteen times in sixteen different keys, without stopping! And it was beautiful. Everyone wanted to know: Who was this kid?

From then on, Benny started playing at nightclubs all over Chicago. Soon everyone was talking about "this amazing kid who plays clarinet." He was only fourteen, playing music with grown men.

But this was a strange life for a boy. Every night, Benny came home from his shows at two o'clock in the morning, his pockets stuffed with dollar bills.

Benny gave this money to his family,
and convinced his father to get an easier
job, working at a newsstand downtown.

But a bad thing happened. Benny's
father was crossing the street, and a car
hit him. He died.

Benny couldn't believe the news.
He didn't know what to say or do. His
father was his favorite person in the
world—and now he was gone. Benny
wished he had thanked his father more for
all his encouragement. But Benny had
never been good at talking. He said what
he had to say through music.

So while his brothers and sisters cried,

Benny played the clarinet. And he kept on playing,

and playing,

and playing,

until everyone in the world had heard his beautiful music.

and playing,

until everyone in the world had heard his
beautiful music.

You can still hear his music. On his recordings, Benny keeps on playing and playing and playing.